# i love it h ▬ ✶

tony watts

Taen

Press

i love it here*
thailand

Text and photography by Tony Watts

Consultant: Sandy Walsh
Designer: Pauline Yong

First published in 2007 by Luxe Life Pte. Ltd.
220 Tagore Lane #03-01
Singapore 787600

Correspondence to:
PO Box 189
Tanglin Post Office
Singapore 912407
contact@loveitthere.com
www.loveitthere.com

Paperstock used in the production of this book is from wood grown in sustainable forests and manufactured using a non-
acid bleaching process. Ink is soy based in an alcohol-free printing solution.

ISBN 978-981-05-8563-1

Printed in Singapore by KHL Pte. Ltd.

# >>contents

# >>introduction

We love Thailand, it is that simple. There are plenty of reasons why this is the case, but every immigration stamp from The Land of Smiles elicits a smile.

There is so much happening in the hospitality industry here that it is difficult to keep track. One – unwelcome – trend seems to be for hotels with loads of style, and loads of attitude to go with it. Those are the properties that don't make this book.

We are looking for style for sure, but also that something extra that makes a visit one that we want to repeat. This sort of honesty is hard to find – we know, because we've spent years looking for it, and that is the reason this series of books was born. This is why we don't accept advertising from hotels or resorts, nor can they pay to be included in these pages.

This book is the result of years of experience, of literally dozens of trips to Thailand – for business and for pleasure – and of more hotel nights than we care to admit. That makes us demanding customers, but it also means we can share our experience. And that is what *i love it here\* - thailand* is all about.

That we were there last week is not important – we are already planning to return.

About the rankings:

Every hotel included is here on merit, but some are better than others.

**lifetime love** – This is the real thing; true love. These hotels are the best you will find, and will keep you coming back.

**lost weekend** – The tumultuous affair. It makes your heart flutter to think about, but it couldn't last forever. These places are not perfect, but pretty close.

**one-night stand** – You know you shouldn't have but it was good, wasn't it? These are the places you might even revisit.

In any case, what's important is that you love it here.

# >>bangkok

Apparently one night in Bangkok can make a hard man humble, but we wouldn't know about that. All you really need to know is that this metropolis of officially around six million – though some estimates put it more than double that – is one of the world's great cities.

Locals know Bangkok as Krung Thep, or 'City of Angels', and while we acknowledge that you can find just about anything here, angels are possibly thin on the ground.

What is rather easier to find is traffic, choking pollution, sleaze, grime, and throngs of people.

And we love the place.

Bangkok is a city of contrasts: temples to traditional deities coexist happily with modern temples to consumerism, in the shape of gleaming shopping malls; expensive European cars sit alongside smoking *tuk tuks* in the ever-present traffic jams; and there is sophistication and sleaze in about equal measure in the thriving bar scene. And the food – from street vendors to slick international restaurants – is amazing.

Plus the hotels here are some of the best you will find anywhere. Stay in Bangkok and you will quickly realise that one night is not nearly enough.

# Sukhothai

It is difficult to know where to start and where to stop singing the praises of The Sukhothai. Leave the berserk Bangkok traffic on South Sathorn Road behind, and enter the far more gracious world of the Sukhothai. In the foyer a centrepiece of fresh tuberoses offers up an intoxicating and welcoming scent.

The rooms feature muted gold silks and the mirrored, wood-panelled bathrooms are brilliant, though it pays to upgrade rooms if you are a bathroom fanatic, as they are substantially smaller in the basic rooms.

Guest rooms are spread over two wings, so the hotel never quite feels as large as the total number of rooms would suggest. Subtle landscaping and architectural details add to the atmosphere of peace and privacy. The open courtyards and long colonnaded walkways offer tantalising glimpses of water features or traditional Thai artefacts.

This is a full-service hotel with all the amenities you would expect at an international standard property, but with a much warmer, more welcoming feel. Even business travellers are well looked-after with high-speed internet connections.

As with everything else, eating is a pleasure at The Sukhothai, with an indulgent breakfast buffet and the renowned Celadon Thai restaurant, which is worth a visit even for those not in residence.

She may not be a youngster but she's still a winner.

## The Sukhothai

| | |
|---|---|
| address | 13/3 South Sathorn Road Bangkok 10120, Thailand |
| phone | +66 2 344-8888 |
| web | www.sukhothaihotel.com |
| capacity | 210 rooms |
| rates | US$300-2,100++ |

### ranking - lifetime love
Do we really have to leave?

### luxe
• Slick design • Brilliant service • Utter serenity in the midst of a frenetic city

### less luxe
• Situated on a ridiculously busy eight-lane road – if you must leave the hotel compound

### best for
Total luxury and a feeling of exclusivity in a city setting.

### ✱ insider tip
Upgrade to an executive suite for loads of room and brilliant bathrooms at only a small premium.

# i.sawan

A six-room property right in the heart of Bangkok may sound too good to be true. And it is – i.sawan is part of the expansive Grand Hyatt Erawan complex. While the Hyatt is one of the better choices in town from the big hotel chains, i.sawan raises things to an entirely new level. The fifth level, if you believe the spiel – apparently i.sawan means 'the fifth level of heaven.'

The villas feature sitting rooms and spa treatment rooms, as well as the expected bedrooms and bathrooms, plus each has a private outside sitting area. The latter would be a nice touch if it weren't for the fact that it is about level with the SkyTrain, which passes by on two sides of the property. But you're not short of space inside the big villas.

As it is part of the spa complex, the fridges in the rooms are stocked with fresh juice, and yogurt and there are Lavazza coffee machines too. Nice.

Finding fault here is difficult – everything is really very well done. You get loads of towels, loads of space, and loads of privacy too. Maybe we should complain about the temptation to stay and luxuriate in the room, rather than getting out and doing anything else.

Fifth level of heaven? Maybe it is.

---

**i.sawan Residential Spa & Club, Grand Hyatt Erawan Bangkok**

address  494 Rajdamri Road,
              Bangkok 10330, Thailand
phone     +66 2 254-1234
web         www.isawan.hyatt.com
capacity  6 rooms
rates       THB20,800++

### ranking - lifetime love

The best address in Bangkok for shopping, plus absolute peace when you retire to the room. It doesn't get better than this.

### luxe

• Loads of space • Privacy

### less luxe

• Pool is shared with guests from the main hotel • Noisy outdoors

### best for

Shop, and then drop into one of these enormous, comfortable rooms.

### ✳ insider tip

Use the main hotel's excellent executive floor facilities – it is part of the deal.

# Metropolitan

There's one problem with being the latest hip spot to see and be seen, and that's that there is bound to be competition not far behind. In this milieu four years may seem like an eternity, but the Metropolitan Bangkok seems to have weathered the ravages of time quite well.

The rooms still look fresh, new and uncluttered, and the restaurants remain at the cutting edge of contemporary.

That's not to say we don't have complaints (of course). The pool is huge, but there's too few seats and no shelter from the weather. The outlook from just about every room is pretty darned ugly. And, rather shockingly, we got some attitude from the staff when dining at the headline restaurant Cy'an – maybe it was just an off night.

There's not much the hotel can do about the tattiness of Bangkok, but it does a good job of the things within its power to make your stay comfortable.

The rooms are sleek, modern and comfortable too, and the bathrooms (and amenities) are up there with the best.

Well worth a look.

## Metropolitan Bangkok

| | |
|---|---|
| address | 27 South Sathorn Road, Tungmahamek, Sathorn, Bangkok 10120, Thailand |
| phone | +66 2 625-3333 |
| web | metropolitan.como.bz |
| capacity | 171 rooms |
| rates | US$240-2,000++ |

### glow all day dining

| | |
|---|---|
| garden vegetable, tomato & barley soup with pesto | |
| chicken, young coconut & shiitake mushroom soup | 200 |
| avocado, seaweed, cucumber & radish salad with japanese dressing | 200 |
| garden greens, leaves & seed salad, ginger miso dressing | 220 |
| glow caesar - baby romaine, avocado, wholewheat croutons | 280 |
| parmesan & tofu aioli | |
| roast pumpkin, beetroot & pepper salad, pine nuts & persian feta | 280 |
| raw marinated black kingfish salad, tomato, chilli, lime & | 320 |
| coriander | |
| blue crab, green papaya, exotic fruit & herb salad, sesame | 320 |
| tamarind dressing | |
| tiger prawn, pomelo & young coconut salad, chilli, lime dressing | 200 |
| spicy shredded chicken salad with spicy cashew nut dressing | 320 |
| vegetable & 7 grain burger, tomato salsa, hummus harissa yogurt, | 210 |
| beetroot & carrot slaw | |
| yellow fin tuna, olive grilled red pepper & egg wholewheat panini | 300 |
| wholemeal flat bread wrap with shredded chicken & glow slaw | 360 |
| fragrant green curry of tofu & vegetable with brown rice | 280 |
| steamed fish of the day in hot & sour broth, lemon basil & brown rice | 340 |
| grilled black kingfish & chickpea salad, sumac dressing & hummus | 600 |
| spiced chicken skewers dried fruit & nut salad, tahini yogurt sauce | 600 |
| glow vegetarian pad thai with brown rice noodles | 360 |
| stir fried brown rice with vegetables, tofu & egg crepe | 200 |
| chilled raw tuna, buckwheat noodle salad, soy & lime dressing | 380 |

### ranking - lost weekend
There is a lot of competition for your hotel dollar in Bangkok, and The Metropolitan is a deserving option.

### luxe
• Style, sweetie • Dining

### less luxe
• Ugly outlook

### best for
Closing the curtains and enjoying a night indoors.

### ✴ insider tip
Eat breakfast at Glow – the hotel's healthy, organic eatery – rather than the main restaurant.

# The Eugenia

We're sorry to say it, but The Eugenia had us fooled; our first impressions were that it was a genuine historic property. Rough-hewn wood flooring and actual antiques will do that. But it is not the case – the building itself is relatively new, just designed to recreate a bygone era.

In most senses it works, though we feel that period style can coexist with all the mod-cons, and The Eugenia does let itself down a little in that sense. Why you would design a small, old-style bathroom if you are starting from scratch is beyond us.

In just about every other sense The Eugenia is a winner though. It's small, in quite a good location, and has a very welcoming feel.

If you're after a Bangkok bolt-hole you could do much worse.

### The Eugenia
| | |
|---|---|
| address | 267, Soi Sukhumvit 31, Wattana, Bangkok 10110, Thailand |
| phone | +66 22 599-019 |
| web | www.theeugenia.com |
| capacity | 12 rooms |
| rates | THB5,800-7,200++ |

## The Eugenia

### ranking - lost weekend
Period ambience done well.

### luxe
• Small • Stylish • Comfortable • Cozy pool area

### less luxe
• A bit far from the SkyTrain • Borders on being stuffy • Small bathrooms • Dead animals on the walls not to all tastes

### best for
A formal, almost European feel, right near the shopping district.

### * insider tip
There's not much outdoor space, making a Junior Suite a better choice.

# Triple Two Silom

**W**hatever Triple Two Silom does, it does it with style. Its long corridors are decorated with original paintings and subtly lit, imparting a cool, quiet air that contrasts completely with the chaotic street outside.

The rooms are surprisingly bright and airy, although the hotel has a limited amount of public space, which means it could start to feel too enclosed after a long stay. A rooftop sitting area would be a nice touch if only it had a plunge-pool for cooling off.

Triple Two has a better street frontage than many hotels on Silom, mainly because it is not under the shadow of the SkyTrain, which diverts away from Silom Road about a block away. While this means the streetfront bar is a nicer place to sit, it does also mean a bit of a hike to the nearest station.

With relatively few rooms, Triple Two Silom feels more inviting than many big city hotels, and the staff actually seem to enjoy themselves on the job, making a stay here a pleasant and welcoming respite.

**Triple Two Silom**

| | |
|---|---|
| address | 222 Silom Road, Suriyawong, Bangrak, Bangkok 10500, Thailand |
| phone | +66 2 627-2222 |
| web | www.tripletwosilom.com |
| capacity | 75 rooms |
| rates | THB5,500-6,900 |

### ranking - lost weekend
Funky address for a Bangkok shopping spree.

### luxe
• Smart design • Quiet rooms, despite the busy road outside • Private • Super friendly staff • Small

### less luxe
• No pool, but you can use the one at the ugly tourist hotel next door

### best for
Shop till you drop, then sit in the bar and watch the world go by.

### ✱ insider tip
Upgrade to a suite, particularly if you are planning a long stay.

# Chakrabongse Villas

Leading the charge when it comes to small guesthouses-turned-hotels in Bangkok is Chakrabongse Villas. Dating back to 1908, the original villa sits inside a quiet walled compound, alongside a pair of traditional Thai teak houses. The three main rooms available are housed in these, though a new two-bedroom suite with Chinese décor is due to open as we go to press.

The Riverside Villa, which features a private deck literally over the Chao Phraya River, is our pick – water views in Bangkok don't get any closer than this.

A member of the Thai royal family owns the guesthouse, so it should come as no surprise that it is walking distance from the royal palace, and it is also across the river from picturesque Wat Arun.

The downside is that while you are close to Bangkok's major tourist attractions, there is little else of interest in the immediate area.

For seasoned Thai travellers the wood-pannelled Lanna-style rooms may be passé (though the Garden Suite features more modern décor), but the location and relative peace and quiet win it for us.

---

## Chakrabongse Villa

| | |
|---|---|
| address | 396 Maharaj Road, Tatien, Bangkok 10200, Thailand |
| phone | +66 2 622-3356 |
| web | www.thaivillas.com |
| capacity | Three rooms |
| rates | THB8,000-15,000++ (seasonal) |

### ranking - one-night stand
Absolute riverfront and absolute escape.

### luxe
• Lock the world outside • Private
• Super friendly staff • Small

### less luxe
• Facilities are available for conference groups • A long way from the shopping, if that's what you are in Bangkok to do

### best for
Leaving the city's busy roads behind and appreciating its river traffic instead.

### ✱ insider tip
The Riverside Villa is the room you want.

# The Davis

Don't be misled by the super slick lobby of The Davis – there is a chance you'll end-up in a room that your aunt from the country might like. Select well though, and things could be different.

The Davis offers a bewildering array of room themes, and not all will be to all tastes. Our Thai style room did little to turn us on, though the Superior room we saw seemed to have it's act together much better in terms of décor, even if the corridor outside is no indication of the style within.

The pool on the rooftop is hardly huge,

but nicely executed, and we managed to have it to ourselves during our stay though it must be said the hotel was at about half capacity at that stage.

In the theme of trying to offer something for everybody, The Davis includes ten Thai-style bungalows at the back of the high-rise part of the hotel, situated around their own quiet pool.

Baan Davis, as this part is known, offers its own check-in desk and two and three-bedroom, two-story residences which are fairly conservatively decorated in a traditional Thai style. If you're travelling with a fat wallet and third wheel then

Baan Davis might be just the thing you're looking for.

Camp Davis, situated next to the hotel, hardly lives up to its name – it is actually a small mall for F&B outlets, such as the ubiquitous Starbucks.

## The Davis Bangkok

| | |
|---|---|
| address | 88 Sukhumvit 24, Klongteoy, Bangkok 10110, Thailand |
| phone | +66 2 260-8000 |
| web | www.davisbangkok.net |
| capacity | 238 rooms, 10 villas |
| rates | THB3,000-15,000++ |

### ranking - one-night stand
Slick and stylish public areas, but occasionally lets itself down with the details, and some rooms aren't so special.

### luxe
• Pleasant rooftop pool area • Lavish Baan Davis residences

### less luxe
• At the wrong end of Sukhumvit 24, so it's a 20-minute walk back from the SkyTrain

### best for
A weekend shopping in nearby Sukhumvit.

### ✱ insider tip
Upgrade to a superior room for smarter design and coffee and tea facilities in the room.

# Dream

Are we dreaming? If Thai-meets-über-modern is your thing, then Dream may well push your buttons – and if not, there's always the bar.

Don't expect to be blown away at the lobby level though – we think they've gone for Phillipe Starck, without much success. Not everybody has the talent to pull together a disparate collection of decorations, and the lobby here looks a bit of a mishmash. And the wall of glass looking out over the fairly ratty-looking side street is a bit of a worry.

Plus the revolving cube at the entrance looks very much like the old Enron one; we hope it's not a sign.

There is good news though. If you're a style-meister then Dream is the latest très modern addition to Bangkok's busy hotel scene, and that may well be enough incentive to book.

The location is quite good  – close to the Sukhumvit shopping strip – so the ingredients are all there for a good stay, with the notable exception of a pool, which is due when the new wing opens in the near future.

## Dream Hotel Bangkok

| | |
|---|---|
| address | 10 Sukhumvit Soi 15, Sukhumvit Road, Kloeng Toey Nua, Wattana Bangkok 10110, Thailand |
| phone | +66 2 254-8500 |
| web | www.dreambkk.com |
| capacity | 100 rooms |
| rates | US230-450++ |

### ranking - one-night stand

It may be too funky for sandals, but Dream is in a dream location for those who shop.

### luxe

• Design • More flat screens than you can point a remote at

### less luxe

• Will probably date quickly
• No pool...yet

### best for

Staying near Bangkok's hottest spots.

### ✱ insider tip

Pay the extra for a Junior Suite – you'll get twice the space of a standard room.

## Stay

**Featured Hotels:**
- Chakrabongse Villa
- The Davis
- Dream Hotel Bangkok
- The Eugenia
- i.sawan Residential Spa & Club, Grand Hyatt Erawan Bangkok
- Metropolitan Bangkok
- The Sukhothai
- Triple Two Silom

Also:

**THE CONRAD BANGKOK**
+66 2 690-9999
87 Wireless Road
Bangkok 10330, Thailand
www.conradhotels.com
A big international brand doing everything right. Slick rooms, efficient service, and one of the best bars in town.

**GRAND HYATT ERAWAN BANGKOK**
+66 2 254-1234
494 Rajdamri Road,
Bangkok 10330, Thailand
www.hyatt.com
Right in the heart of the action, the Grand Hyatt is a great choice for a big city hotel. Fork out extra for the club floor.

**THE ORIENTAL BANGKOK**
+66 2 659-9000
48 Oriental Avenue,
Bangkok 10500, Thailand
www.mandarin-oriental.com
Great riverfront setting, but the rooms are not exciting unless you can afford the Authors' Suites in the old part of the hotel.

**THE PENINSULA BANGKOK**
+66 2 861-2888
333 Charoennakorn Road, Klongsan,
Bangkok 10600, Thailand
www.peninsula.com
Some would say The Peninsula is on the wrong side of the river, but a free shuttle boat takes care of that. River views from all rooms, which are stylish but overly wood-panelled.

## Eat

**AGALICO**
+66 2 662-5857
20 Sukhumvit Soi 51, Bangkok, Thailand
This all-white conservatory-style tea-room is a strange find in downtown Bangkok. Strange also is the fact it's only open from Friday to Sunday afternoons. Tea and scones anyone?

**CELADON**
+66 2 344-8888
The Sukhothai Hotel, 13/3 South Sathorn Road, Bangkok 10120, Thailand
www.sukhothaihotel.com
Part of the Sukhothai Hotel, Celadon is in a stand-alone building overlooking a lily pond. Despite an extensive menu, the food is always exceptional.

**CY'AN**
+66 2 625-3333
27 South Sathorn Road, Tungmahamek, Sathorn 10120, Bangkok, Thailand
metropolitan.como.bz
The Metropolitan's headline restaurant serves up imaginative Mediterranean-inspired meals in a slick poolside setting. Try to book a poolside table.

**EAT ME**
+66 2 238-0931
1/6 Piphat Soi 2, Bangkok, Thailand
Really smart restaurant in a side street off Convent Road. It is small, so you will probably need to book ahead. Excellent service, imaginative food and a decent wine-list. A winner.

**GREYHOUND CAFÉ**
+66 2 664-8663
2nd Floor, Emporium Shopping Complex, Sukhumvit Soi 24, Bangkok, Thailand
Part of a chain, the Greyhound Café in the Emporium is one of the bigger and better offerings and perfect for a break from the shopping. Western-style comfort food is a welcome bonus.

**MAHA NAGA**
+66 2 662-3060
2 Sukhumvit Soi 29, Bangkok, Thailand
For modern Thai cuisine, served with style, Maha Naga is hard to beat. The stunning conversion of an old villa offers separate dining rooms around a central courtyard.

**SPRING AND SUMMER**
+66 2 392-2757
199 Soi Promsi 2, Sukhumvit 39, Bangkok, Thailand
For casual dining Spring and Summer is a welcome respite, though it isn't quite within walking distance of the Sukhumvit shops. Spring is a Thai restaurant, Summer a chocolate-themed café, set around a yard in a pair of rennovated retro houses. Very pretty at night.

## See

**THE RIVER**
You will feel like a tourist – if you're reading this you probably are – but do hire a long-tail boat for a trip along Bangkok's klongs. It is well worth the effort. You get to see a side of Bangkok life that is visible no other way, as well as enjoying transport not affected by the city's notorious traffic. A fascinating and relatively peaceful activity.

**THE ROYAL PALACE**
The royal palace in Bangkok is a worthwhile diversion. You will have to fight the bussed-in hoards of tourists, so start early and remember to cover up as bare shoulders, midriffs and legs are frowned upon.

**DIZZYING DRINKS**
For pre-prandial drinks with a view there are two brilliant options – Sky Bar at the Dome at State Tower (www.thedomebkk.com), and Moon Bar on top of the Banyan Tree Bangkok (www.banyantree.com). If it rains on those parades – they are both completely exposed to the elements – head for the smooth sophistication and live band at the Diplomat Bar at the Conrad instead (www.conradhotels.com).

**BARGE ON INN**
Stay overnight on a converted rice barge and cruise to Ayutthaya, a UNESCO World Heritage Site. This is about the most pleasant way to experience life on the Chao Phraya river, and you get to explore the ruins in the ancient Thai capital at the end. Try the more luxurious of the two Manohras (www.manohracruises.com), or the less glamorous Mekhala.

# >>chiang mai

The unofficial capital of the north is one of our favourite places to visit in Thailand. It is a relatively quiet provincial centre with a huge number of picturesque temples inside the crumbling walls of the original town.

The city has grown beyond those walls and moat of course, but it has done so while retaining a great deal of character. You are as likely to walk around a corner and find a golden stupa glinting in the sunlight as a boutique selling home-grown fashion.

There is the usual tourist tat available too – check out the night market for highly amusing printed tee-shirts and knock-off handbags – but, being the centre of the Lanna Kingdom, expect to find some truly interesting handicraft too.

Plus, you can actually catch a *tuk tuk* here without choking to death on exhaust fumes, and not feel like a tourist doing it – the locals actually use them to get around as well.

Probably Chiang Mai is not the best option if you want the hottest bars and clubs, but the city has charm, and that alone makes it a worthy destination.

# The Chedi

If Chiang Mai city is your destination there is no doubt that The Chedi is the address to have. Chiang Mai may feel like a country town on occasion, but The Chedi injects a welcome dose of metropolitan polish.

The location – on the city side of the Mae Ping River – is difficult to beat, and some clever architecture helps render the noise from the busy street outside nearly inaudible.

The rooms are in an L-shaped, four-storey building, which forms a courtyard with the river and the service areas as the other boundaries. Many rooms offer views out over the river from their large balconies, though the high floors are the pick and, as the majority face the courtyard, the ones at the end of the 'L' have a better outlook.

Overlooking the river in the centre of the block is a spa, a historic bungalow – formerly the British consul's residence – and a stunning, lily-fringed lap pool. Unfortunately the pool was overrun with screaming children when we visited, and there is simply nowhere to escape to in this circumstance – unless you're staying in a Chedi Club Suite.

The tariff may be 50 per cent higher than the Deluxe Room, but you get twice the space, as well as access to the excellent club floor, a proper coffee machine in the room, and an inclusive mini-bar.

Money well spent.

Thanks to The Chedi we are already planning to return to Chiang Mai.

---

**The Chedi Chiang Mai**

address    123-123/1 Charoen Prathet Road, T. Changklan, A. Muang, Chiang Mai 50100, Thailand

phone    +66 53 253-333

web    www.ghmhotels.com

capacity    84 rooms

rates    THB11,400-17,200++ (seasonal)

### ranking - lifetime love
All the excuse you will need to go to Chiang Mai.

### luxe
• Slick design • Great service
• Surprising serenity • Good restaurant

### less luxe
• Mosquitos • The pool can be overrun with screaming children

### best for
A city break with a resort feel.

### ✱ insider tip
The suites are enormous, and entitle you to use the club floor facilities. Suites 223, 323 and 423 offer the most privacy.

# The Rachamankha

Too many hotels endeavour to make your stay a predictable one. There are times when you could be anywhere in the world – in a room with generic décor, in a building of generic design, and with generic service. How meaningful is it when everyone flashes a smile and tells you to "have a nice day"? We like to think of those as hotels for the McDonald's generation.

The Rachamankha is exactly the opposite, and that is entirely welcome.

The hotel is laid-out to mimic the chapel of a temple, with most of the rooms arranged around two interconnecting courtyards, and other buildings and the pool accessible through passages off the main courtyards. It is a marvelous way to maximise the limited space available, making you want to wander all the paths and explore.

The rooms are hardly enormous, and the bathrooms are too small, but the décor – with genuine antique furniture – is pleasant. This taste of Lanna style is appropriate given that the Lanna kingdom was based in Chiang Mai.

The hotel's location is perfect too; inside the walls of the old city, and only a short walk from the city's most visited temple, Wat Phra Singh.

Not that there isn't plenty to keep you occupied in the hotel itself. Genuine art and antiques line the walkways, and there's even a small gallery, which is well worth visiting. Plus, the restaurant – set around a courtyard – is another draw.

For a genuine taste of northern Thailand, The Rachamankha should definitely be on your list.

## The Rachamankha

| | |
|---|---|
| address | 6 Rachamankha 9, T.Phra Singh, Chiang Mai 50200, Thailand |
| phone | +66 53 904-111 |
| web | www.rachamankha.com |
| capacity | 24 rooms |
| rates | THB5,500 - 7,900 (seasonal) |

### ranking - lost weekend
Lanna style without the kitsch.

### luxe
• Peace and privacy • Central location
• Surprisingly nice pool area

### less luxe
• Service is willing, but can be hit or miss
• Small bathrooms • Basic room facilities

### best for
Staying in the old part of town and enjoying the peace.

### ✱ insider tip
Spare some time to enjoy the pleasant pool area.

# Tamarind Village

**B**uilt around a massive tamarind tree, the 40 rooms and three suites at Tamarind Village offer a comfortable, peaceful stay in the middle of Chiang Mai.

Since our last visit the hotel has been renovated, which means some welcome changes – particularly to the previously disappointing bathrooms. Also a spa has been added to the equation.

The rooms themselves are not the largest, and there are arguably too few public sitting spaces, but otherwise Tamarind Village gets just about everything right.

It certainly manages a lot of style: from the bamboo-lined drive to the white orchids in the reception. And it is small enough that even after a short stay, you will feel like part of the family.

Tamarind Village might not be a destination in itself, but for exploring the old part of Chiang Mai, it is easily one of the best choices.

**Tamarind Village**
address  50/1 Rajdamnoen Road,
Sri Phom, Muang,
Chiangmai 50200, Thailand
phone  +66 53 418-896/9
web  www.tamarindvillage.com
capacity  45 rooms
rates  THB4,200-12,600++ (seasonal)

# Tamarind Village

### ranking - lost weekend
Rustic but stylish.

### luxe
• Pretty at night • Peaceful • Small

### less luxe
• Pool area could be larger • Often fully booked

### best for
A stylish base from which you can explore Chiang Mai on foot.

### ✱ insider tip
The suites are certaily nicer, but for the budget-conscious the Lanna rooms are mighty good value.

# dusitD2 chiang mai

Why is it that 'affordable' usually means 'without any style'? Fortunately nobody seems to have told the Dusit group that's the case, if the dusitD2 chiang mai is any indication.

What you get here is a good dose of modern style, at a price you're going to like. And the hotel is located where the city's night-bazaar operates – though that may not prove so tempting for frequent travellers, as it seems to include all the regular night-bazaar tat. Still, if you want to explore Chiang Mai town, it is a good location.

There is only one restaurant and one bar in the hotel – though a meal at Moxie is recommended, with the caveat that the Thai dishes are the best on the menu. But again, being in the right locale means plenty of other choices nearby.

The basic rooms are fairly small, so we'd suggest the Studio Suites if you suffer hotel-room claustrophobia. The Club Deluxe tariff entitles you to use the club lounge, so that may prove a worthwhile investment for the small price premium over the regular Deluxe rooms if you're on a tighter budget.

As the D2 is in a renovated building the pool area is not particularly impressive, though the gymnasium on the top floor offers views over town while you sweat.

It may not offer the ultimate in luxury, but the D2 is a good stylish choice in the heart of Chiang Mai.

## dusitD2 chiang mai

| | |
|---|---|
| address | 100 Chang Klan Road, Tambol Chang Klan, Amphur Muang, Chiang Mai 50100, Thailand |
| phone | +66 53 999-999 |
| web | www.d2hotels.com |
| capacity | 131 rooms |
| rates | US$154-513++ |

### ranking - one-night stand
Location, style and substance, and at the right price too.

### luxe
• Close to the shopping • Back from the main road, so relatively peaceful

### less luxe
• Standard rooms can feel cramped
• Average pool

### best for
A weekend of shopping in the heart of Chiang Mai city.

### ✱ insider tip
Upgrade and get access to the club lounge.

# Four Seasons Resort Chiang Mai

Until recently, the Four Seasons Resort Chiang Mai had a monopoly on high-end accommodation in northern Thailand, and in some senses the incumbent seems to have been resting on its laurels.

Still, the resort has plenty to offer. Clustered in groups of four, 64 Lanna-style Pavilion Rooms surround a terraced valley that the hotel uses to cultivate rice. The two-storey duplex buildings offer salas for each room along short walkways, although they are not quite as private as we would like.

The rooms are tasteful, but the décor does give away its 1995 origins, with woodwork that just looks very 1990s. Still, nothing was falling apart or looking tatty during our visit.

On the opposite side of the valley from the rooms are the three-storey Residences, offering guests the choice of the ground floor, with it's own plunge pool, or the upper two floors, which are three-bedroom penthouse suites.

If you really must do something, there is a cooking school to keep you busy, but otherwise the big draw is the spa.

The treatment suites here have to be seen to be believed, and there is a huge range of massages, body scrubs, facials, and packages available. You may well need a soothing massage after seeing the pricing, however.

And that's the rub at the Four Seasons Chiang Mai. The location is away from town, but it is pretty, with views over the rice terraces and manicured gardens towards a distant mountain range. And everything here works too. Just expect to have to pay for the privilege.

## Four Seasons Resort Chiang Mai

| | |
|---|---|
| address | Mae Rim-Samoeng Old Road, Mae Rim, Chiang Mai 50180, Thailand |
| phone | +66 53 298-181 |
| web | www.fourseasons.com/thailand |
| capacity | 80 rooms |
| rates | US$475-4,000++ |

## Four Seasons Resort Chiang Mai

### ranking - one-night stand

A full-service resort with everything you would expect from an international hotel chain.

### luxe

• Massive residences • Amazing spa
• Cooking school

### less luxe

• Pricing • Looking a bit dated
• Not exactly close to anywhere special

### best for

Lock yourself away for a couple of days pampering and learn how to make your favourite Thai meal.

### ✱ insider tip

Ask for a room away from the open-air cooking school – some participants can get raucous.

# At Niman

At Niman is one of the quirkier choices in Chiang Mai. The eight rooms are decorated in a South Asian style 'inspired by the impression of cultural inheritable of the Himalayas through the great mountain of Chiang Mai – Doi Suthep', or so says the hotel's literature.

Confused? Think of it more as a house decorated with Nepalese and Indian furniture and lanterns, endowing it with an almost Moroccan feel.

You enter through a garage – it was being used to display hand-woven carpets when we visited, though it is as often used as storage for motorcycles – and up a flight of stairs, were you arrive at a small courtyard with a tiny pool, sitting areas, and two of the eight rooms, including the one photographed here.

Further flights of stairs connect you to the other six rooms over two levels. Each is decorated differently, and most offer at least some outdoor seating, though there isn't much of a view from any of them.

Still, the guest house (you couldn't really call it a hotel) is on a quiet street, and around the corner from some really interesting boutiques on the Nimmanhaeminda strip.

For the most part the rooms are comfortable, and while you can't expect polished service, the staff seem more than willing to help, even when the language barrier makes things a little difficult.

Downstairs – next to the entrance to the garage – is La Muang de Cusine Snob, the hotel's small restaurant, offering an imaginative northern Thai menu.

At Niman is not everyone's cup of ginger tea, but for something different at a reasonable price it is worth a look.

---

**At Niman Conceptual Home**

| | |
|---|---|
| address | 37 Soi 9 Nimmanhaeminda Road, T. Suthep A. Muang, Chiang Mai 50200, Thailand |
| phone | +66 53 224-949 |
| web | www.aaitaam.com |
| capacity | 8 rooms |
| rates | THB4,000-6,000 |

## At Niman

### ranking - one-night stand
A quirky mix of styles that comes together remarkably well.

### luxe
• Willing staff • Small size • Friendly

### less luxe
• Small pool • More a guest house than a proper hotel • We suspect wear and tear will be a problem in the long term

### best for
Avoiding the crowds and indulging in some shopping for local wares.

### ✱ insider tip
Rooms vary rather wildly in size and style – ask to see another if you're not happy.

## Stay

Featured Hotels:
- At Niman
- Chedi Chiang Mai
- dusitD2 chiang mai
- Four Seasons Resort Chiang Mai
- The Rachamankha
- Tamarind Village

Also:

### BANN TAZALA
+66 53 850-111
55/5 Moo 1 Chiangmai-Sankampaeng Road, T. Tasala, A. Muang, Chiang Mai 50000, Thailand
www.banntazala.com
They don't get much more boutique than this. Squeezed onto a long, narrow block, Bann Tazala makes the most of its limited space with interconnecting courtyards and eight stylish rooms. It is directly opposite the Mandarin Oriental (see below) which means about 10 minutes drive to get to Chiang Mai city.

### MANDARIN ORIENTAL DHARA DHEVI
+66 53 888-888
51/4 Moo 1 Chiangmai-Sankampaeng Road, T. Tasala, A. Muang, Chiang Mai 50000, Thailand
www.mandarinoriental.com
Disneyland comes to Thailand. The Mandarin Oriental Dhara Dhevi recreates a Lanna Kingdom city, with villas in clusters around rice fields, a colonial wing (Thailand wasn't colonised by the British, but let's not split heirs), and a spa that is supposed to be an exact replica of a Burmese palace. The style is a little over the top for our tastes, but the restaurants here do a fine job.

## Eat

### GINGER CAFÉ
+66 53 419-014
199 Moon Muang Road, T. Sriphum, A. Muang, Chiang Mai 50220, Thailand
Arguably the best place in town for a casual café style lunch, or just a break from the shopping – except of course that it is part of a shop. Expect sandwiches and salads, a good selection of cakes, and friendly service, all in a bohemian drawing-room setting.

### THE HOUSE
+66 53 419-011
199 Moon Muang Road, T. Sriphum, A. Muang, Chiang Mai 50220, Thailand
Right next door to Ginger Café (see above), The House is a more formal eatery, set over two levels in an old villa. The cuisine is international, combining some Asian and western elements, and the wine list is decent – read affordable by Thai standards – too. There is a tapas bar attached which is good for lighter meals.

### LE GRAND LANNA
+66 53 888 888
51/4 Moo 1 Chiangmai-Sankampaeng Road, T. Tasala, A. Muang, Chiang Mai 50000, Thailand
www.mandarinoriental.com
This is where the Mandarin Oriental Dhara Dhevi all started – as a stand-alone restaurant on the outskirts of town. The setting is rather lovely – in a cluster of traditional houses with a large alfresco deck area. You will get a cultural performance, but it is worth putting up with because the cuisine is the star – it is some of the best Thai food we've had anywhere. It may be a trek to get there, but it is worth the effort.

## See

### OLD TOWN
The charm of Chiang Mai is that it is a city of temples. There are literally hundreds within the walls of the old city. Get your walking shoes on and explore.

### WAT PHRA THAT DOI SUTHEP
Chiang Mai's most sacred temple is about 15 kilometres out of town, on a hill with commanding views over the city. There are a lot of steps to climb to get to the temple – though you can pay to take a tram up. It isn't Thailand's biggest Buddhist temple, but it is impressive, with its golden stupa. It is one of the more visited sites in the area, so expect crowds and hawkers.

### CHIANG RAI
There's no need to stay in Chiang Rai if you want to get to the Golden Triangle – where Thailand meets Burma and Laos at the confluence of the Mekong and Nam Ruak rivers. It can be done as a day trip from Chiang Mai. To be honest the journey itself is more interesting than the destination – Sop Ruak town caters almost entirely to the backpacker crowd. Still, if you're tired of the city and want to take in some countryside scenery you could do worse.

# >>koh samui

Palm-fringed beaches may sound like clichéd notions of paradise, but a visit to Koh Samui is enough to have you forget your cynicism, particularly if there's a longtail boat bobbing in the blue water adding an exotic element to the scene.

Koh Samui is our favourite Thai beach destination. The development has been kept somewhat in check by building regulations that limit the height of structures near the beach – nothing is supposed to be above coconut-palm level – but there is still enough to keep an international visitor happy.

There is a good selection of luxe hotels and decent restaurants, but still a village atmosphere. And the airport is one of our favourites anywhere for its casual, laid-back atmosphere – hopefully the new terminal being pressed into service now will retain that.

Chaweng is the main tourist centre, and it can seem overrun, but it does have its charms, and other parts of the small island are well worth exploring too.

Mainly though, Samui is about chilling-out, and doing it in style.

# Sila Evason Hideaway at Samui

When the Evason group says hideaway, it means hideaway. The Sila Evason Hideaway is on a peninsula on the northern tip of Koh Samui, occupying an entire headland.

There is a reasonably pleasant beach at the eastern side of the resort although you have to negotiate a fairly steep path to get there. But why bother when chances are there is a pool in your villa compound as well as a fantastic main pool on top of the hill?

You probably will not want to drag yourself away from your villa at all. The rooms have views out over the ocean, plenty of areas to sit and read a book, and enormous bathrooms, some with views from the bathtub.

We have stayed on several occasions, and find it difficult to fault the rooms – some offer more privacy than others, but each has had its plus-points.

The rustic décor is just like that at other Six Senses resorts, so you could experience Evason fatigue if you have been to a few. If not, some of the details like the handmade light fittings are surprisingly imaginative.

The Thai food here is brilliant – not watered-down for western palates – but we find the western fare just a bit too fussy. And we didn't seen the need for a jazz duo in the restaurant, when the sound of the waves below was as much music as we needed.

Still, these are minor points, the Evason remains our favourite Samui getaway.

### Sila Evason Hideaway & Spa at Samui

address    9/10 Moo 5, Baan Plai Laem, Bophut, Koh Samui, Surathani 84320, Thailand
phone    +66 77 245-678
web    www.six-senses.com
capacity    66 villas
rates    THB15,000-181,000+++ (seasonal)

### ranking - lifetime love
Great villas. Great service. Great location.

### luxe
• Spacious rooms • Service extras
• Brilliant Thai food

### less luxe
• Disappointing western food
• Some villas' pools are less than private

### best for
Locking yourself away in rustic luxury.

### ✳ insider tip
Try the free daily activities such as yoga or pilates.

# The Library

Book 'em, Danno. It is no crime to be the literary type at The Library – the hippest address on Koh Samui's busy Chaweng beach.

Bearing no resemblance to the site's former use as a backpacker bungalow resort, The Library's 26 rooms line the edges of the deep block, leaving a grassy, open area in between.

At the beachfront the red-tiled pool sits between the resort's funky gymnasium, restaurant, and library.

The rooms are comfortable, and minimalistic, and the design works quite well. The room is bisected by a plinth, on which sits a daybed and the regular mattress, though the latter is squeezed against a wall on one side. Bathrooms in the lower level Suites have spa baths, but otherwise we'd be opting for the more private Studio rooms above, which offer much the same space for less money.

It is also a shame that the amenities here – in the bathrooms and otherwise – are more reminiscent of a motel. There is simply none of the imagination applied to the mini bar that was applied to the overall design, for instance.

Still, there is no other comparable resort in Chaweng. Sit on one of the poolside beanbags and you'll see an astonishing number of people stop to wander in to have a look. Fortunately the security staff keep the hoi polloi at bay.

Thanks to the Library you can call us bookworms.

## The Library

| | |
|---|---|
| address | 14/1 Moo 2, Chaweng Beach, Bo Phut, Koh Samui, Suratthani 84320, Thailand |
| phone | +66 77 422-767 |
| web | www.thelibrary.name |
| capacity | 26 rooms |
| rates | THB9,000-13,500+++ (seasonal) |

Please Do Not Disturb

Please Do Not Disturb

### ranking - lost weekend
Friendly, funky; fantastic.

### luxe
- Design • Children are discouraged
- Pool area • Location • Relative peace

### less luxe
- Bathrooms not as fab as bedrooms
- Incredibly bright library lights can kill the mood in the restaurant

### best for
Easily the best address on popular Chaweng beach.

### ✽ insider tip
Choose the cheaper Studio rooms – they are more private and have more natural light than the Suites.

# Sala Samui

Call it the Goldilocks syndrome. We are difficult to please on most counts, and location is one of the big ones. Not all beaches are created equal, and while we like the private ones, in Thailand they don't legally exist; all beaches here are public, and the pretty ones tend to be more public than others.

As with Goldilocks all we want is 'just right.' In this context Sala Samui is onto a winner. Choeng Mon beach is pretty enough, but not overrun with people. It is also home to a number of backpacker-type bungalow resorts, which means there are some really decent and cheap

beachfront restaurants too – Honey Seafood at end of the beach is one of our all-time favourites.

That's not to say that Sala Samui doesn't get the food and beverage side of things right; if you avoid the theme nights the restaurant is really quite good, and the setting is special too.

Accommodation-wise Sala Samui is an odd one for Thailand – the concept is almost Balinese, with walled compounds and private pools, though the architecture is definitely Thai. And it works.

The rooms are comfortable, private, and difficult to leave. We like the Sala

Pool Villas for their relative value, though the Pool Villa Suites (pictured) are more spacious and have a more open feel.

From a value perspective Sala Samui is difficult to beat, and the location is a winner too. Call it just right.

---

**Sala Samui Resort and Spa**

| | |
|---|---|
| address | 10/9 Moo 5, Baan Plai Lam Bo Phut, Koh Samui Suratthani 84320, Thailand |
| phone | +66 77 245-888 |
| web | www.salasamui.com |
| capacity | 69 villas |
| rates | US$260-1,110++ (seasonal) |

### ranking - lost weekend
Private pool villas on a pleasant beach.

### luxe
• Location • Private compounds • Two stylish main pools

### less luxe
• Theme nights at the restaurant • Pools can get crowded

### best for
A taste of Samui's beaches without too much tat.

### ✱ insider tip
Sala Pool villas offer the best compromise between space and price.

# Four Seasons Koh Samui

**F**our Seasons is one of the latest additions to the Koh Samui hotel scene, and is at the vanguard here when it comes to the big hotel brand names. In some senses this is a good development; it means international service standards, for one thing. It also means that the position isn't Samui's very best – all the most spectacular spots on the beach have been taken.

There is a small stretch of sand here, but it is not the most fabulous beach on the island. And, more importantly, the resort is a fair distance from Samui's other attractions. So if you intend to explore the island you're in the wrong spot.

The villas are well designed with this in mind; there is loads of space – both indoors and out – so you will never feel claustrophobic. The rustic design touches, such as the bannisters made with logs and ropes didn't do it for us, but the villa has everything you want, including an iPod dock, an outdoor minibar, a huge bathtub and a sensationally comfortable bed.

Also there is a decent daybed under cover on the deck, which has curtains that can be drawn for extra privacy. Nice.

The Four Seasons Koh Samui is in a pretty enough setting and the villas are attractions in themselves. If you aim to lock yourself away for a few days you could do worse.

## Four Seasons Resort Koh Samui

| | |
|---|---|
| address | 219 Moo 5, Angthong, Koh Samui, Surat Thani 84140, Thailand |
| phone | +66 77 243-000 |
| web | www.fourseasons.com/thailand |
| capacity | 60 villas, 2 residences |
| rates | US$600-2,300++ |

## ranking - lost weekend
Villas with the lot.

## luxe
• Get the right room, and you are guaranteed privacy • Loads of outdoor living space • Very competent service

## less luxe
• Some rooms are much less private than others • Steep paths mean going everywhere by golf buggy • High food and beverage pricing

## best for
Staying locked away in your villa

## * insider tip
Avoid villas in the 300s, which are the least private. Villas at the end of the roads get less passing traffic.

# Renaissance

Are you a Renaissance man? We find ourselves in two minds: it is part of our mission to find well-rounded hotels and resorts, but is the Renaissance Koh Samui Resort & Spa one of them?

In some senses it does set out to please everybody. The resort is built across a relatively quiet sidestreet. On the beach side of the road there are villas (pictured) with their own plunge pools and sun decks, while on the other side of the road are the deluxe rooms in a six-storey wing.

While we like the villas, there is a lot to be said for the deluxe rooms; the ones on the upper floors have views out over Lamai Bay; they have spa baths on the decks; and the pool on this side of the road is nicer and quieter than the one on the beach side.

Then again we are suckers for villas with private pools, even if the décor doesn't really do it for us, as is the case here.

Location-wise the Renaissance is okay; between Chaweng and the increasingly popular Lamai stretch, and the hotel provides shuttle-bus services to both.

While the beach at the resort is pretty, there is little else within walking distance, so if a trip to Thailand must include finding beachside restaurants this might not be the place. Still, the Renaissance is a well-rounded option.

## Renaissance Koh Samui Resort & Spa

| | |
|---|---|
| address | 208/1 Moo 4, T. Maret, Laem Nan Beach, Koh Samui 84310, Thailand |
| phone | +66 77 429-300 |
| web | www.marriott.com |
| capacity | 33 villas, 45 rooms |
| rates | THB5,900-38,000++ (seasonal) |

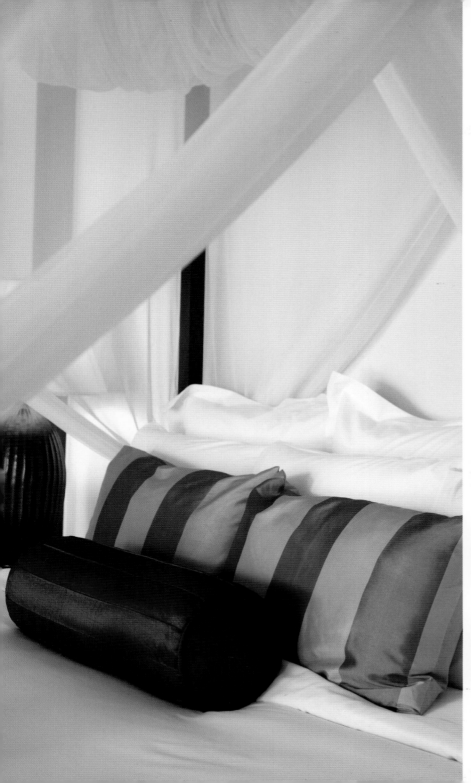

### ranking - lost weekend
A big name brand hotel chain with a small property in Samui.

### luxe
• Everything works • TawaNN was one of the best restaurants on the island, though there is a new chef now • Pleasant beach • Choice of pools

### less luxe
• Some villas are not very private • Décor not to all tastes

### best for
A full-service experience without the dizzying pricetag.

### ✱ insider tip
Deluxe rooms are good value.

# Villa Nalinnadda

All the ingredients are in place to make Villa Nalinnadda a really great property: it is small, it is set on a quiet stretch of beach, and the design is attractive too.

With all these boxes checked we were set to love the place, but there are a couple of flies in the ointment.

Firstly, the hotel backs onto the main road that encircles the island. To be fair the traffic tends to get quiet after 8pm, and it is not an expressway, but it does start up again fairly early, and if the sound of vehicles passing on a consistent basis upsets your delicate sensibilities it may well drive you insane.

Secondly, while the property enjoys absolute beachfront, the beach itself is not particularly fabulous, and there's really not much of interest to see if you do choose to take a walk on the sand.

Also, if you're a bathroom aficionado, the basic items on offer here are unlikely to ring your bell – ours served as the entry to the room. Strange.

So then what is Villa Nalinnadda doing in these pages? Because waking-up in the all-white room, and looking out past the coconut palms at the exotic long-tail boats on the clam water was quite a magical experience.

Yes, you are going to have to overlook the fact that the curtains don't block any of the light, and that you will probably hear some traffic noise, and that breakfast isn't that special.

It is flawed, but if you have your own transport, and aren't there for an extended period of time, Villa Nalinnadda is a quaint option.

## Villa Nalinnadda

address   399/1-4 Moo 1 Maret,
          Koh Samui 84310, Thailand
phone     +66 77 233-131
web       www.nalinnadda.com
capacity  8 rooms
rates     THB5,800-9,900 (seasonal)

### ranking - one-night stand
A small, friendly and relaxed option, away from Samui's busier beaches.

### luxe
• Views from room balconies • Few guests makes for tranquillity • Not very child friendly

### less luxe
• A long way from any tourist attractions, such as restaurants • Not on a swimming beach • Noise from the main road • Some rooms' bathrooms are very odd

### best for
Chilling out without the crowds.

### ✱ insider tip
The beachfront room has the best views and one of the better bathrooms.

## Stay

Featured Hotels:
- Four Seasons Resort Koh Samui
- The Library
- Renaissance Koh Samui Resort & Spa
- Sala Samui Resort and Spa
- Sila Evason Hideaway & Spa at Samui
- Villa Nalinnadda

Also:

### AMARI PALM REEF RESORT & SPA
+66 77 422-015
Chaweng Beach, Samui 84320, Thailand
www.amari.com

Okay, it's a big tourist resort, but the position is good, and the bar is quite funky. Make sure you get a room on the beach side of the road, and be aware that the water in front of the resort gets shallow and hot at times.

### KARMA SAMUI
+66 77 234-500
80/32 Moo 5, Bophut, Koh Samui, Suratthani 84320, Thailand
www.karmasamui.com

Good Karma? With one- to four-bedroom pool villas all with ocean views you'd have to say yes, though they are a bit close together for our tastes.

### LE PARADIS BOUTIQUE RESORT & SPA
+66 77 239-041
101/1 Moo 3, Chaweng Beach, Bophut, Koh Samui, Suratthani 84320, Thailand
www.leparadisresort.com

The choice of 14 contemporary villas or 12 traditional Thai teak villas makes Le Paradis an intriguing option. The tranquillity in this part of Chaweng is refreshing too. Shame the pool is so small.

### EDEN ROCK VILLA
+66 77 413-552
211/5 Moo 4 Maret, Koh Samui, Suratthani 84320, Thailand
www.edenrok.com

Think villa, rather than hotel (check-out Villa Beige in the 'And Also' chapter), but there is not necessarily anything wrong with that. Eden Rock is perched on one of the steepest hills we've ever driven up, but has sweeping views out over Chaweng Bay. The Rice House accommodates four, but is comfortable for two as well, and very private.

## Eat

### THE CLIFF BAR & GRILL
+66 77 414-266
124/2 Tambon Maret, Lamai Beach, Koh Samui, Thailand
www.thecliffsamui.com

Mediterranean food in a pleasant setting looking out over a peaceful bay. The food is hardly cutting-edge innovative, but the terrace is a great place to while away a couple of hours over lunch. Take a careful look at the large rock just below and you'll see why it's known as the elephant stone.

### THE FIVE ISLANDS
+66 77 415-359
348/3 Tambon Taling Ngam, Samui 84140, Thailand
www.thefiveislands.com

We don't care that The Five Islands is a trek right across the other side of the island, this is a professionally run, smart Thai eatery that just happens to have the best sunset views on Samui. A memorable experience.

### PREGO
+66 77 422-015
Chaweng Beach Road, Samui 84320, Thailand
www.prego-samui.com

Prego is actually run by the Amari Palm Reef Resort diagonally across the road, but don't let that put you off – this is casual Italian done very well indeed. The setting is very pleasant, the service attentive, and the food authentic.

## See

### WATERWORLD
Samui is really all about the beaches. You can choose to just lie around on them, or try a day trip on a sailing vessel and look at the beaches from the other direction.

### LOCAL LIFE
Despite the tourists and the development there are still quaint, original villages around the island. Wander through Fisherman's Village on Bophut Beach in the north – there are actually some original wooden Chinese shop-houses standing. Some of the original inhabitants, by the look of it too. The story is much the same in Hua Thanon on the east coast, with its Muslim community and market.

# >>phuket

**P**huket is arguably Thailand's most developed tourist destination. This means that access is easy and infrastructure is in place, so it makes a relatively gentle introduction for first-time Thailand visitors.

That the island has some of the most beautiful natural scenery you will find anywhere helps, though quiet, unspoiled beaches are things of the past – giant resorts abound.

Still, Phuket and its surrounds are home to some of Thailand's most luxurious lodgings. We would advise you avoid Patong Beach – Phuket's often trashy main torurist centre – and head for the slightly quieter environs further north.

Plus, it is the stepping-off point for Phang Nga Bay, where quiet unspoiled beaches do exist – though it helps to have a boat to get to them.

Don't expect to find too much in the way of the rustic rural lyfestyle anywhere in Phuket – shopping malls and even traffic jams are more likely – but the island will have you dreaming of return journeys.

# Trisara

Interior design prizes are one thing, and completely sorted resort experiences another. We sincerely doubt Trisara is about to score a gong for the former, but that is a matter of taste – Trisara gets everything else right.

The location is fantastic to begin with. It is close enough to the airport to make transfers a breeze, but it is seemingly miles from Phuket's rampant development.

Villas are spread around a natural ampitheatre, with the ocean as the focalpoint – every villa gets views of the ocean and the sunset.

That said, not all are equal. Trisara is one of those places where you really need to upgrade rooms. The Ocean View Pool Suites are nice enough, but the Pool Villas are in another league entirely, and while the price is higher, it is easy to justify. If you don't do the Pool Villas here you really are missing the point.

The point that Trisara doesn't miss – that too many others do – is that there is more to running a hotel than a pretty location and smart design. The service standards here set the bar for others to follow.

And for foodies, the restaurant is excellent too. We wanted to stay longer, just to try some more menu items. How often can you say that?

If substance is important to you, then Trisara is your sort of place.

---

## Trisara
| | |
|---|---|
| address | 60/1 Moo 6 Srisoonthorn Road, Cherngtalay, Thalang, Phuket 83110, Thailand |
| phone | +66 76 310-100 |
| web | www.trisara.com |
| capacity | 42 villas and suites |
| rates | US$745-1,850+++ (seasonal) |

### ranking - lifetime love
Incredible ocean views, slick service, and brilliant villas. Winner.

### luxe
• Everything works • Great restaurant
• Pleasant beach • Stunning main pool

### less luxe
• Décor not to all tastes • Nothing much else nearby

### best for
The best of Phuket.

### ✱ insider tip
The Pool Villas are the only way to go.

# Evason Hideaway

# at Yao Noi

The latest in the ever-expanding Evason Hideaway portfolio is on the quiet island of Yao Noi in Phang Nga Bay just off Phuket. That the island seems so quiet and rural is something of a surprise, given its proximity to the bustling tourist destinations of Phuket and Krabi, but it is entirely welcome.

It does mean there isn't much else to do on the island, but even a leisurely tour is worth the time — the main economic activities are fishing, rubber tapping and rice cultivation, all of which are done in old-fashioned labour-intensive ways that are sure to disappear.

What you are more likely to do is close the doors to the enormous room and stay there — particularly if you stop to calculate the per-hour rate you're paying.

Still, our villa had more daybeds than we could get around to using, a private plunge pool — with absolutely stunning views — and even views from the bathtub.

While we have some lingering doubts that the butler arrangement works well, the location, the food and the size of the villas win it for us. We didn't want to leave, and that's the point, isn't it?

### Evason Hideaway at Yao Noi

| | |
|---|---|
| address | 57/5 Moo 1, Tambol Koh Yao Noi, Amphur Kho Yao, Phang-Nga 82160, Thailand |
| phone | +66 76 418-500 |
| web | www.six-senses.com |
| capacity | 56 villas |
| rates | THB21,300-84,000++ (seasonal) |

## Evason Hideaway at Yao Noi

### ranking - lost weekend
Incredible villas in a stunning and quiet location.

### luxe
• Lock the world outside • Friendly staff
• Good food • Smooth transfer by car and speedboat from Phuket

### less luxe
• Pricing is very high • Some villas not as private as they could be

### best for
Quiet contemplation of life...of the pool, of the beach and of the menu too.

### ✱ insider tip
Hang the expense – you want an ocean-view villa.

# Twinpalms Phuket

At first sight, we thought Twinpalms was another of those too-cool properties that are more about style than substance. A resort hotel in Phuket that is not on the beachfront? Surely they jest.

But Twinpalms makes up for its location in several ways. First, it is only a two-minute walk from Surin Beach – one of the prettiest and least spoiled on the island. (Be sure to have a meal at one of the beachside shacks – it is one of the highlights of Phuket.)

Second, it has a casual beach club area, so guests can enjoy the sun and the sand, as well as indulge in some light meals or cocktails while staring at the ocean. Nice.

Our main beef is that the one pool can get crowded, but the beach club rescues that somewhat. We were disappointed to find the amenities we enjoyed previously have gone, however.

While the rooms are quite small and too close together for completely secluded privacy, Twinpalms is well worth considering if Phuket is your destination and you're on a budget.

### Twinpalms Phuket

| | |
|---|---|
| address | 106/46 Moo 3 Surin Beach Road Cherng Talay, Thalang Phuket 83110, Thailand |
| phone | + 66 76 316-500 |
| web | www.twinpalms-phuket.com |
| capacity | 76 rooms |
| rates | THB5,900-60,400+++ (seasonal) |

Twinpalms Phuket

## ranking - lost weekend

A small, funky hotel in Phuket without painful pricing – wonders will never cease.

## luxe

- Great beach almost on the doorstep
- Interesting shops and restaurants within easy walking distance • Smart beach club

## less luxe

- Not close enough to the beach for sea views or the sound of the waves
- Starting to look a bit tatty in places
- Can be lots of children in the pool

## best for

A stylish taste of Phuket.

## ✱ insider tip

The hotel's main restaurant, Oriental Spoon, is popular with local residents, and for good reason – the food is good and the pricing reasonable too.

149

# Amanpuri

High-end luxury in Asia was practically invented by Aman, and Amanpuri is where it all began. The stunning property was the first ever Amanresort, celebrating its 20th birthday in 2008.

Don't make the mistake of thinking this makes it old and tired – as we go to press it is receiving a birthday treat of a bit of a spruice-up, but the Pavilions look as fresh today as many of their contemporaries, and that's before the make-over.

They do show their age in one respect: in this price-bracket the expectation is to have a private pool with the room, but that is about the only flaw we can find with the Amanpuri. You can always lash-out on one of the Villas if you absolutely cannot live without a pool of your own.

As Aman was the first to stake its claim here, the location is a stunner – the resort occupies an entire peninsula covered with mature coconut trees, and has a pristine stretch of private-access beach.

Another very pleasant beach is shared with a neighbouring resort.

Where the Amanpuri stands out is in its experience – 20 years of looking after demanding guests has made for a seamless experience that many of the pretenders can't come close to matching.

Amanpuri is apparently a Sanskrit word meaning 'place of peace.' We are at peace including it here.

## Amanpuri

| | |
|---|---|
| address | Pansea Beach, Phuket Island 83000, Thailand |
| phone | +66 76 324-333 |
| web | www.amanresorts.com |
| capacity | 40 pavilions, 30 villas |
| rates | US$525-7,850++ (seasonal) |

### ranking - lost weekend
Stunning location and seamless service.

### luxe
• Everything works • Great food • Truly friendly service

### less luxe
• *Mon dieu!* No pools in the Pavilions • Price of the Villas • Pavilion salas could be more private

### best for
Discovering what a difference years of experience can make.

### ✳ insider tip
Wander off to nearby Surin Beach for a cheap local seafood meal.

# The Racha

If you want to get away from it all, The Racha is your sort of place. Getting there can be a bit of a chore, particularly if the weather is rough, as it is on Koh Racha Yai, an island 20 kilometres south of Phuket. You could spend an hour on a speedboat bobbing around like a cork. We did. And that's on top of a fairly long car transfer – the jetty is about as far from the airport as you can get in Phuket.

But the location could not be prettier – on a well-protected bay that is popular with divers and snorkellers. The white walls of the Racha contrast starkly with the stunning blue sky, green foliage, and aquamarine water.

It is not all roses in paradise: the rooms could be more private and the service was friendly but a bit lacklustre during our visit; the lights were so unfathomable that we ended up leaving them on all night in the sitting room of our pool villa; and the food could be improved.

Also, the floating jetty at the island was quite challenging.

The Racha scores points for style though, and if some of the little niggles could be fixed, it would be one of the better destination hotels in Thailand.

## The Racha
| | |
|---|---|
| address | 42/12-13 Moo 5 Rawai, Muang Phuket 83130, Thailand |
| phone | + 66 76 355-455 |
| web | www.theracha.com |
| capacity | 70 rooms |
| rates | THB5,700-60,000+++ (seasonal) |

### ranking - one-night stand
Superb beach and stylish villas.

### luxe
• Location • Style

### less luxe
• Transfer can be rough • Needs more substance to go with the style, particularly with service and food

### best for
Getting away from Phuket.

### ✱ insider tip
Beachfront villas are the best by a fair margin.

## Stay

Featured Hotels:
- Amanpuri
- Evason Hideaway at Yao Noi
- The Racha
- Trisara
- Twinpalms Phuket

## Eat

### AMANPURI
+66 76 324-333
Pansea Beach, Phuket Island
83000, Thailand
www.amanresorts.com

You can get a taste of the Aman magic – literally – by eating there. Dine alfresco by the wonderful pool at the Terrace and experience food and service as they should be done.

### BAAN RIM PA
+66 76 340-789
223 Kalim Beach Road, Kathu,
Patong, Phuket 83150, Thailand
www.baanrimpa.com

A Phuket institution. Baan Rim Pa has been packing them in for years. The Thai cuisine is competent, but the view – looking down on Patong beach (a habit of ours, it must be said) – is what keeps the punters coming back. Go for dinner – Patong looks much better with the lights sparkling on the water, and you're less likely to notice the fairly ordinary décor.

### ORIENTAL SPOON
+ 66 76 316-500
106/46 Moo 3 Surin Beach Road, Cherng Talay, Thalang, Phuket 83110, Thailand
www.twinpalms-phuket.com

Twinpalms' smart eatery offers Thai and Italian flavours, and a chilled-out ambience. Sunday brunch is popular with Phuket residents.

### THE BOATHOUSE WINE & GRILL
+66 76 330-015
Kata Beach, Phuket 83100, Thailand
www.boathousephuket.com

Boathouse Wine & Grill at Mom Tri's Boathouse is a good beachside option. Particularly so if you enjoy your wine – the Boathouse is consistently recognized for its 700-bottle wine list. Cuisine is Thai and Mediterranean.

### TRISARA
+66 76 310-100
60/1 Moo 6 Srisoonthorn Road,
Cherngtalay, Thalang, Phuket
83110, Thailand
www.trisara.com

Not only does Trisara get everything right with its accommodation, but.the dining is an experience too. Thai and international flavours and impeccable service. A winner.

### WATERMARK
+66 76 239-730
The Boat Lagoon 22/1 Moo 2 Thepkasattri Rd., Muang, Phuket 83000, Thailand
www.watermarkphuket.com

Mod-Oz cuisine in a smart setting next to some boats you can't afford. It is a trek to get there, but not a bad way to finish a day out on the water.

## See

### PHANG NGA BAY
Because of the rampant development on Phuket there is often the desire to get away from it all, and doing so on a boat on Phang Nga Bay is the ultimate way to do it. The scenery is stunning, the water relatively protected, and there is a very good chance you will find that which is missing on Phuket island – a deserted beach. The good hotels operate their own fleets, or check out www.sunsail.com, or www.tawancruises.com.

### KRABI
There are other ways to get away from Phuket – the simplest is to go by car. Krabi and Koh Lanta (see 'and also') are both accessible by car, though the latter is a fairly long drive with several car ferries on the way. Still, it is the best way to get there short of a private boat, and the scenery along the way can take your breath away.

# >>and also

So, you want to get off the beaten track in Thailand? And you want luxury? It can be done. In fact there's too much to include in one book, but we've chosen some of the more interesting options that don't require days of extra travel time.

Generally you will choose the north for cultural experiences and the south for beaches, though we don't mean to imply there's no culture in the south. And really, does riding an elephant truly count as a cultural experience?

What we have done is include some experiences that really are worth the extra travel time, plus, as private villas are becoming more commonplace in Thailand, one of those for good measure. With the exception of the villa, these 'and also' properties are best accessed via smaller regional airports, so the travel time – particularly for long-haul visitors – is possibly going to be prohibitive.

It is an esoteric selection, in some out-of-the-way destinations too, but if anything it does show that there is more depth to Thailand than just the main tourist centres.

# Costa Lanta

The sleek, sparse, unadorned bungalows at Costa Lanta mark a dramatic departure from the usual Thai resort. Twenty polished-concrete and unfinished wood structures dot the rear of Costa Lanta's large beachfront plot. Most have walls that open to allow the sea breeze into the bedroom with its mosquito-netted double bed.

A waterway snakes through the property, crossed by footbridges that give access to the beach, restaurant and pool. Unfortunately, the water can get stagnant at certain times of the year.

The design is the main attraction here, although sometimes style takes priority over substance. The big doors on the standard rooms can be hard to open and close, and it feels like you are sleeping in a garage with the doors closed. For this reason, we would choose one of the four more user-friendly Superior rooms.

The rooms are architecturally attractive, but the lofty restaurant and bar is the focus of the resort. Subdued lounge music sets the scene, without drowning out the lapping of waves. The Thai food is excellent, although the service is often at a slow island pace. Massive doors are permanently open for the cooling sea breezes.

With only 22 rooms and a large block, you never feel crowded at Costa Lanta, although more vegetation between the rooms would add to the privacy. The giant new resort being built next door could affect the relative peace of Costa Lanta, but it is difficult to guess how much.

For the style conscious, Costa Lanta stands alone: way too cool.

## Costa Lanta

| | |
|---|---|
| address | 212 Moo 1, Saladan, Amphur Koh Lanta, Krabi, Thailand |
| phone | +66 75 684-630/2 |
| web | www.costalanta.com |
| capacity | 22 rooms |
| rates | THB3,025-10,780 (seasonal) |

### ranking - lost weekend
At times, too groovy for its own good but unlike anything else you will find.

### luxe
• Slick design • Cool pool • Right on a pretty beach • Few guests makes for tranquillity • Not very child friendly • Value • More sun-loungers than guests

### less luxe
• A long-haul trip from anywhere and there are no genuinely luxe ways to get there • Tap water can smell awful – and you will be showering in it • High prices at peak times

### get there
Krabi airport is the closest, though it is still a fair drive, and Phuket is about four hours by road. Avoid the public ferries.

### best for
Chilling out in style.

### ✱ insider tip
Take a superior room for a more comfortable experience.

# Rayavadee

You can't help but be overwhelmed by the stunning scenery on arrival at Rayavadee, and better still, the boat drops you off at the most disappointing of the three Rayavadee beach frontages. The other two are even more spectacular.

If you wrote a wish list of natural features to build a resort around, you could not do better than this.

Rayavadee's individual villas dot a coconut plantation that is dwarfed by massive jungle-clad limestone formations. Phra Nang Beach in particular is breathtaking and probably the most photographed beach in Thailand.

The downside is that easy boat access from Ao Nang means the beach is often overwhelmed by day-trippers. The resort handles this well by providing private decks overlooking the sand and keeping the general public out.

Architecturally, the villas are a bit of a concern, dotting the landscape like a bunch of giant mushrooms. But they are functional, comfortable and difficult to leave when the time comes. However, the swinging bathroom doors and so-so water pressure could be fixed.

Another quibble: the Thai meal we tried was a little disappointing.

Overall, though, it is hard to fault Rayavadee. From the smooth transfers, to the welcoming service, to the seemingly endless touches to make you feel welcome, Rayavadee fulfils its promise. The stunning location is a bonus.

## Rayavadee

| | |
|---|---|
| address | 214 Moo 2, Tambol Ao-Nang Amphur Muang, Krabi 81000, Thailand |
| phone | +66 75 620-740 |
| web | www.rayavadee.com |
| capacity | 102 pavilions |
| rates | US$ 524-3,189++ (seasonal) |

## ranking - lost weekend
If you are alive and breathing, this place will impress you.

## luxe
• Spacious and quiet rooms • Stunning scenery

## less luxe
• The pool is showing its age • Décor will not please all tastes

## get there
Krabi airport is about 30 minutes by road, and there's a short boat transfer. Phuket is another airport option, but expect to spend a couple of hours driving.

## best for
Lazing around on one of the world's most spectacular beaches and watching the sun go down from the extraordinary Grotto Bar.

## ✱ insider tip
Spa and Hydro Pool Pavilions offer more private outdoor areas than the Deluxe Pavilions.

# Aleenta

**B**outique is possibly the most overused word in the hotel marketers' jargon, but with only seventeen rooms Aleenta Resort and Spa can truly lay claim to the word.

Five rooms are on the retaining wall on the beach, and of these, the Pool Villas are our pick, although none are as private as you might like. Five more rooms are housed in a three-storey structure behind the single-storey Pool Villas, offering sea views from the second-floor rooms and penthouse above.

Pak Nam Pran beach is not one of Thailand's prettiest beaches, but it is quiet, so if you want a relatively undisturbed time, Aleenta might just be the right place. Unfortunately, it is a long three- to four-hour drive from Bangkok, making it difficult to get to.

Being located right on the shoreline makes maintenance an issue, but it does mean peace and quiet given the almost deserted beach. Don't expect to discover much local colour here – there is very little to see within walking distance.

Small bathrooms and a lack of wardrobe space aside, Aleenta gets just about everything right. If you want to get away from Bangkok for a weekend escape, it is one of the better choices.

---

### Aleenta Resort and Spa, Hua Hin Pranburi

| | |
|---|---|
| address | 183 Moo 4, Paknampran, Pranburi, Prachuabkirikhan 77220, Thailand |
| phone | +66 2 508-5333 |
| web | www.aleenta.com |
| capacity | 17 rooms |
| rates | US$129-317++ (seasonal) |

### ranking - lost weekend
Only ten rooms in the main hotel and no children under 12 – a policy for true serenity.

### luxe
• The welcoming and personal service you can only get in a place this small

### less luxe
• Not the greatest beach in Thailand
• Bathrooms are too small

### get there
Hua Hin airport has only limited service, the other option is a road transfer from Bangkok.

### best for
Listen to the waves lapping the shore while digesting a good book.

### ✱ insider tip
Go for a Pool Villa with uninterrupted water views and its own outdoor spa pool.

# Villa Beige

Thailand is starting to take Bali on in the private villa stakes. It used to be that if you wanted to get together with some friends in South-East Asia and rent a full-service villa, Bali was about the only choice, but the proliferation of swanky private villas in The Land of Smiles means there's been a shift of late.

And places like Villa Beige can make you see why that is – it has style in abundance if you go for the *Austin Powers* retro look. And if you get together with a group of friends the pricing seems reasonable too. Who gets the master bedroom in the main house may make for some discord, however – it is the best of the four rooms.

And why is it, we wonder, in a villa that accommodates eight, there were only four loungers by the pool when we arrived?

Still, what you get here – as with other villas – is a great opportunity for privacy with a group of friends. Not many other villas have a million-dollar outlook like this one does, however.

In that respect we'd argue that Villa Beige is a more colourful choice than its name implies.

---

**Villa Beige**

address   70/1 Moo 3 Tumbon Taling
          Ngam, Koh Samui, Thailand
phone     +66 77 234-419
web       www.villabeige.com
capacity  4 rooms
rates     US$1,200-2,000++ (seasonal)

## ranking - lost weekend
Villas offer the ultimate in privacy.

## luxe
• Sensational views • More personal space than a hotel

## less luxe
• Some rooms are better than others

## best for
Party in privacy with a group of friends.

## ✱ insider tip
The Five Islands Restaurant – our favourite on Koh Samui – is a short drive away.

# Four Seasons Tented Camp

Yes, it is a row of tents, and yes, it is camp. That is if you think *Out of Africa* safari style doesn't really fit in northern Thailand. But the safari theme does make the Tented Camp unique in these parts, and as there is a heavy emphasis on elephant conservation you can forgive some of the interesting décor.

We were shocked to find elephant tusks as door handles but it turns out they're actually resin replicas – it would have been nice to know this was the case rather than having to ask. And if sleeping under canvas isn't your thing, don't worry, we're talking hardwood floors, en suite bathrooms and ducted air-conditioning.

Plus the views from our tent – and the outdoor shower – were of golden stupas in the distant hills of Burma. Very exotic.

It's intention is to be an experience, so expect some stage management (you're ferried down a river in a small boat to arrive at the property, while your luggage goes by road, for instance).

And because it is so small, there is an element of interaction with the other guests at meal times. But the food is sensational; Thai and western set menus, with some choice, and a lot of imagination. We give it the vote for the best resort cuisine we've had in Thailand. And the wine is inclusive.

Plus there is mahout training – a half-day exercise during which you will learn some basic commands for steering an elephant.

If you're willing to pay for the Tented Camp experience you will be impressed.

---

**Four Seasons Tented Camp
Golden Triangle**

| | |
|---|---|
| address | PO Box 18, Chiang Sean Post Office, Chiang Rai 57150, Thailand |
| phone | +66 53 298-181 |
| web | www.fourseasons.com/thailand |
| capacity | 15 tents |
| rates | US$1,557++ |

### ranking - lost weekend
Safari style in the north.

### luxe
• Fantsatic food, and it is included in the price • Views out over Burma and Laos • Inclusive activities

### less luxe
• Minimum three-night stay • Pricing

### get there
Fly into Chiang Rai and transfer by road, or drive from Chiang Mai.

### best for
Seeing the Golden Triangle in style.

### ✱ insider tip
Try the unique wine cellar.